THE NOISE OF A FLY

The Noise of a Fly

DOUGLAS DUNN

FABER & FABER

First published in 2017
by Faber & Faber Ltd
Bloomsbury House
74–77 Great Russell Street
London WC1B 3DA

Typeset by Hamish Ironside
Printed and bound in Great Britain by Bell and Bain Ltd, Glasgow

A CIP record for this book is available from the British Library

ISBN 978–0–571–33381–3

2 4 6 8 10 9 7 5 3 1

Acknowledgements

My grateful thanks are owed to the editors and sponsors of the following publications and anthologies: *Archipelago*; *Dark Horse*; *Dundee New Writing*; *Edinburgh Review*; *Guardian*; *Heav'n Taught Fergusson*; *Jubilee Lines*; *Neu Reekie*; *New Poems Chiefly in the Scottish Dialect*; *New Writing Dundee*; *NHS Glasgow and Greater Clydeside*; *Northern Garden*; *On Shakespeare's Sonnets*; *Peninsula*; *Ploughshares*; *Red Wheelbarrow*; *Scottish Review of Books*; *Spectator*; *TLS*: *Il Tolomeo* (Venice).

Also to the chapbooks *A Whisper to the Muse* (*Un Bisbiglio alla Musa*) (Edizioni di Bradipo, 2008), and *Invisible Ink* (Mariscat, 2011).

Several other poems appeared in *Second Wind: New Poems by Douglas Dunn, Vicki Feaver and Diana Hendry* (Saltire Society, 2015, sponsored by the Baring Foundation).

Contents

When we consider with a religious seriousnesse the manifold weaknesses of the strongest devotions in time of Prayer, it is a sad consideration. I throw my selfe downe in my Chamber, and I call in, and invite God, and his Angels thither, and when they are there, I neglect God and his Angels, for the noise of a Flie, for the ratling of a Coach, for the whining of a doore; I talke on, in the same posture of praying; Eyes lifted up; knees bowed downe; as though I prayed to God; and, if God, or his Angels should aske me, when I thought last of God in that prayer, I cannot tell: Sometimes I finde that I had forgot what I was about, but when I began to forget it, I cannot tell. A memory of yesterdays pleasures, a feare of to morrows dangers, a straw under my knee, a noise in mine eare, a light in mine eye, an any thing, a nothing, a fancy, a Chimera in my braine, troubles me in my prayer. So certainly is there nothing, nothing in spirituall things, perfect in this world.

JOHN DONNE

THE NOISE OF A FLY

Idleness

Can you hear them? The flap of a butterfly.
The unfolding wing of a resting wren.
The sigh of an exhausted garden-ghost.
A poem trapped in an empty fountain pen.

'Wondrous Strange'

Now it can almost be heard. But not quite
Almost. Still on the far side of nearly,
It is the melody of a floating feather.

A spiderweb tickles my cheek in the dark garden;
A briar plucks at my sweater.
Wind on a windless night wafts through my hair.

Or the aroma of sandalwood soap
When that's impossible. Or of fenugreek,
Or the scent of one who is no longer here.

Or something I half-believe I've seen,
A glisk of movement on the hill's horizon,
An ominous shadow cast by nothing at all.

Then there's the taste of zero-flavour,
Not even the taste of my own mouth,
Neither sweet and delicious, or bitter or sour.

Or the taste of strawberries *Romanov*
(That restaurant in Bonn!) or stolen plums
Remembered on a January night when snow's falling.

Is this just dream-stuff, or is there enough
Sense in the senses for the mystical
To prove itself real as any truth?

Yes, it's 'wondrous strange'; but I must ask
My Muse to save me from contriving
A forger's touch of moonlight on the page.

Cognitive Disorders

'Butterflies rock no cradles, nor do they sing.'
Or so a gaga poet writes down on his page.
'I've listened, looked; can't hear or see a thing
Other than snails on their silky pilgrimage
Over the slippery slabs of a garden path.
I've heard ants' martial marching songs,
Their tiny tambourines, trumpets, and gongs,
Too-whoos of the nocturnal polymath.
I've heard the patient moans of mushrooms growing
Where bees coax ding-dongs from a foxglove's bells,
A spider crooning at its loom, sewing
Its webs of death and dinner, bat-squeaks
In moon-shadow, their flittermouse farewells.
Now, though, I'll go and whisper lullabies
To the traceless powdered butterflies
And all the little creatures that die in secret
Beyond imagination, mind, and wit.'

A Teacher's Notes

Forbid morbidity. Time passes.
There's no necessity for sorrow,
Unless . . . Be active. Banish *alases*.
Force no more yawns; and ponder the sparrow.

Don't go out of your way to be improper –
You already are. Grow herbs on windowsills
(If you have them). There's no eavesdropper
On one who works alone, counting syllables,

Saying your lines aloud. Please, not on a train,
Or on a bus, or strolling down the street,
And never, never, *never* on a plane.
And 'twixt and 'tween and o'er *are* obsolete.

So, cherish solitude for the sake of your songs.
Only your Muse, whoever She or He may be,
Your secret listener, pointing out your wrongs,
Your rights, can criticise your poetry.

Think in pictures. Think in rhythm. Then let
Others see and hear them too. Don't forget
Poetry can oblige you to be insolent –
Be so, if that is what you want.

Better still, attend to all five senses.
Make readers see, hear, taste, touch, and smell
Until your poem's narrative convinces
By what's disclosed, and casts its spell.

Live for that secular epiphany
That happens anywhere, that is lying to hand;
But beware the fraudulent and phoney
In anything you cannot understand.

Two years in a garret did no one harm
(And maybe not much good) but you'll get nowhere
Unless you take a risk and chance your arm.
Avoid too much indoors, though. Take the air.

Now, disregard everything I've written.
Turn everything I've said into what you say –
I know you're well and truly smitten.
You'll stay the course, but there's a price to pay.

And, for God's sake, learn how to cook.
No more pot noodles on the hoof!
Until you're famous, keep off the hard stuff.
If you've a mind to, send me your first book.

The Wash

So much time wasted wanting to be remembered
Ends with desire to be forgotten,
As one chirrup absent from the dawn chorus,
An unclaimed seat in the theatre,
A volume missing from the library shelf.

Ambition determines you, then trips over itself;
But I was never a self-lover, or a self-hater.
Is it age that creates this feeling, to bore us,
Or twisted self-knowledge gone rotten,
Or dreams allowed to be dismembered?

I look at the spring's predictable daffodils
Bugling yellow silences, snowdrops and crocus
Already gone, fritillaries abloom,
Tulips, bluebells and others still to come,
And summer's lilies, lupins, and roses.

And all the rest of them, florals and edibles,
And all the rest of botanical hocus-pocus
In seasonal wonder, marguerites, delphinium,
Periwinkles to be pressed in a slim volume,
Honeysuckle, marigolds, whatever Hortus proposes.

It all depends on the luck of the weather,
As everything else does, in a sense,
And everyone. It all comes out in the wash?
H'm. But it could be in someone else's favour,
With the gale and the sleet in your girning face.

Better off forgotten, like scorched heather,
Your weathered and withered intelligence,
Your talent thinning like hair, maladroit tosh
Set down in a notebook as if to savour
Another stab at despair and disgrace.

It's odd how ambition stumbles, and falls,
As the young overtake you, with a pat on the back,
If you're lucky, a smile from over the shoulder.
I did that too. Or I suppose I did.
No harm intended; it's just the way it is,

The way of the world, with its doors and its walls.
Is this all because I've no Muse in my sack?
I don't feel like Sisyphus, I feel like his boulder –
Something used, or abused, for a task that's not ended,
That won't be, and certainly not with this.

So, fall off a barstool swigging your hemlock
For what we have here is perseverance's tedium.
The bowler's seven feet tall and very fast,
Their striker kicks like a camel and you're in goal,
Their scrum-half's fleet-footed as destiny.

Don't worry. Your reputation's safe with me,
Old pal of mine, shadow, my friend, old chum.
How long does a book, or sheet of paper, last?
If the answer is hundreds of years, does that console?
Go early to bed and outstare the clock.

The Nothing-But

He was beginning to live in the region of truth
– GRAHAM GREENE, *The Honorary Consul*

Slowly the truth dawns, the nothing-butness of it,
The fly in the dram, the flea in your ear,
Just-cleaned window now smeared with dove-shit,
Confidence that turns into abject fear,
The niggle, the virtuous irritant,
A taste like garlic, chilli, or mint.

To have kissed the lips of one who was dying
Is to have tasted silence, salt, and wilderness,
And touched the truth, the desert where there is no lying,
Only that kiss and the keeping of its promise.
Who lives there, in that land of the utter truth?
Is it one of the delusions of youth,

Or the delusions of age and adulthood?
Well, I don't know. Only the truth will do,
I suppose, not would, or should, or could,
But what was, and is. Is it the same for you?
As the French say, 'reconstruct your virginity',
In search of beginnings and tranquillity.

The Glove Compartment

After her stroke, hers was the first to go.
It sat for two years in their garage, though,
All through the months of her recovery,
Though that was far from full. Vocabulary
Re-emerged, but slowly. So he retired
A few years earlier than anticipated.
He couldn't leave it all to the nurse he'd hired;
She said he shouldn't, but that's what he did.
'Please, sell my car. I'll never drive again.'
It seemed as final as a sung *Amen*.
He knew it must happen, but didn't know when.

When he opened her glove compartment
He found small change, lip salve, tissues, receipts
From shops and filling stations, peppermint,
An ice-scraper, lipstick, and boiled sweets,
Two tickets for a play at Dundee Rep
(Unused), all sorts of trivial stuff.
He shoved them in a bag. Sat back and wept.
There's love in the world. But never enough.

Remembering Friends Who Feared Old Age and Dementia More than Death

Even when just the other day
From Then to Now feels decades away.
The name at the back of the mind . . .
What can I say?
That memory's fickle, that fretting
Over a lost name or forgotten month
Makes you feel guilty, mindless, and blind,
That it's perfectly natural to fear the labyrinth
Where the 'ageing process' might one day take you
Into the land of forgetting?
You said it, friends. Too true.

Dictionaries become indispensable?
There's an urge to reread the Bible?
That song was in *what* key?
Over the hill,
Round the corners, round the bends,
And *nuts* to you, too, as I check my diary
For wherever it is I'm supposed to be,
Today, or the next, that old clock-sorcery
I don't depend on, though I know I should,
And which you overdid, old friends.
No, I don't think you did,

Not now I'm older. No one
Looks forward to being old and alone,
The carer with a spoon,
Visitor gone,
Boredom and fright on television.
How do you understand the merry young
As you endure a dragging afternoon
With a hundred names on the tip of your tongue,
Unable to cheer yourself up,
In a constant state of indecision?
Cheers! Let's pour another cup.

Recipes and Refugees

I knew a student had a slogan in her car
And BORN TO SHOP, it said. Yes, BORN TO SHOP.
I'm in Tesco's. I wonder where you are.
In Harvey Nick's, or going over the top
In Jenner's with a plastic card? Poets' Day –
Piss Off Early, Tomorrow's Saturday.

I like Friday. I like the supermarket's
Bewildering choice, so much to eat and drink,
Or clean with. *Or, or, or* . . . The deficit's
Enormous in a glimpse, a single blink
That sums up plenitude and liberty,
Tyrannical famine, fear, and poverty.

How can a man be good, and kind, and true,
While knowing he's got more than many have
In hot, dry countries? What can I do?
Or you? Or you? It isn't very brave
To keep on shopping, though to stay alive
Means buying drink and dinner. I'll survive

Even worse torments of guilt and conscience.
Everyone else does. So, then, why can't I?
It feels worse being older, ever since
Remembering when there wasn't much to buy
Or cash to pay for the necessities.
Though not forgotten, these are far off days.

Affluence in exotic recipes –
The choice of what to cook is international.
I welcome that, but think of refugees
Drawing their water from a flyblown well
In the lands of falafel and couscous
Where sympathy is worse than useless.

I hope you've lost your shopper's selfish boast.
In our domestic daily lives, we choose,
We purchase, and we try to make the most,
Morally, of fish, salad, basmati, booze,
Pasta, olive oil, the occasional chop.
It's not just you. Everyone's BORN TO SHOP.

Thursday

Gave yet another lecture. God, I'm boring.
Said all the same old things I've said before
With touches of 'however-ing' and 'therefore-ing'.
Dear God, it's true, I'm just an ancient bore.

If only I could tap my old exuberance,
High spirits that I plied in days before,
Then maybe I would find a kind deliverance
From the curse of being such a bloody bore.

For I'm the model of a modern academic.
I'm absolutely super at ennui.
I'm just stunning when it comes to a polemic,
And boredom's snoredom's what I guarantee.

I'm putting extra pennies in my pension.
Retirement beckons and the garden calls,
That beautiful, botanical dimension
Where boiler-suited pensioners scratch their balls.

But I've a problem. It's called 'work ethic', so
I'll slog on with the daily, dreary toil.
Heigh-ho, heigh-ho, what a lousy way to go,
To work all day then burn the midnight oil.

Leaving the Office

for Frances

Somehow it all gets done and over with –
The office emptied of its archival dross,
Papers re-read, and chucked, the years of breath
Re-breathed, moment by moment. Why feel cross
At this departure? Why feel worse than sad
For fag-ashed, faded memos, decisions taken,
Or not taken, the good, indifferent, bad,
Right ways of doing, and the mistaken?

Permit no tears, but still, allow a sigh
Closing a door on what was once my life,
My days, my work. Farewell, and so goodbye
While haar is forming over North East Fife.
It's like *The Cruel Sea*, the ship going down –
Jack Hawkins with his duffel-coated frown.

'Confidential books over the side? Carry on.'
We should have lit a bonfire on the lawn,
Thrown on the lot. Instead, my Number One
Lugs binbags to the shredder, day by day,
As slow as patient archaeology.
Shiver me timbers! But it's not much fun.

Not pushed, but oh-so-very-gently shoved
Towards the book-loaded van and a pension,
Then shelving shadows with the books I've loved.

Senex on Market Street

'Thou that art now the world's fresh ornament'

Posh totty totter past on serious heels.
In handsomeness, with confidence, they walk
Towards exams, and don't know how it feels
To hear the fateful tick-tock of the clock.
Young women, and young men, I, too, was young –
Believe that if you can! – but years go by
Until, one day, you find your songs are sung;
Ambitionless, your sap and tears run dry.
There's something I must tell – need you know this? –
I loved a woman who dressed as well as you;
But I can't give the past false emphasis,
For even old love is for ever new.
    When she walked out she dulcified the air;
    And so do you. To say so's only fair.

Poem for a Birthday

I still can't get over that lousy conjurer,
All thirty quid's worth of rank incompetence.
It wasn't yesterday. Eleven years since,
Almost to the hour. That slipshod sorcerer,

Butter-fingered wizard . . . Remember, when
No kids applauded as each trick misfired,
And he didn't notice? Then did it again,
Again, and laughed it off, tittered, perspired,

Wiping his brow, until his grand finale
When the white rabbit shat on his shaking hand,
And made a break for it? Don't shilly-shally,
Bunny-boy. Run for it. We'll understand.

You deserve a magician. We all do.
And that fake pencil-line moustache, which fell off?
Don't be like him. Just you be true to you.
Do what you do, my son. It'll be enough.

Botanics

Multicoloured clothes pegs on the line
Are tiny tropical birds hanging upside down.
Their songs are all imaginary.
The tree peony's a candelabrum,
Botanical flame-holder. Maples speak
Native American languages, a eucalypt
Aboriginal Australian, Pieris
A secret tongue of the forest. Magnolia –
Which I don't have although a neighbour does –
Discusses Missisippi in a Dixie drawl.
Ranks of *en garde* gladioli speak
Byzantine Greek, roses Babylonish
And other floral tongues, while quince
Talks Arabic, and an azalea is
A chatterbox in Hindi and Chinese.
Lilies whisper across continents
In secret, erotic dialects
That baffle botanical philologists.
Crab apple – good for jelly – it speaks
Weathered and salty Atlantic lingos,
Survivors' syntax. Spare a thought
For currants, strawberry, raspberry, gooseberry,
Indigenous desserts, mother-made jam,
For lilacs, elder, and the evergreens,
For the big library of tree poetry
In botany's symphonic chorus.

Rookery

A leaf impersonates a pecking bird
And thrashed roses struggle on the frame.
Hooded snowdrops are white whispers,
An archive of anniversaries
And massed crocus an imperial rug.
A month ago
Runic birdprints tracked the frozen snow.

Rooks colonise a tree next door.
There are crow-boudoirs in my fragrant eucalypt.
They suffer from urgency and bad publicity,
Old wives' tales and superstitions.
They are birds of ill omen only to those
Convinced by omens ill or good.
They make a soundtrack for the silhouettes
    of a March dusk.

I prefer the small republics of finches,
Tits, robins, wrens, blackbirds, thrushes, sparrows,
The far-off woodpecker, ghostly owl,
A prayerful tree of doves,
To their corvine autocracy,
Their treetop tyranny
And pitiful aggressiveness.

I can't keep my eyes off them, or ears –
Single-mindedly
Touching down on stick nest engineering,
Their high tree-villages, on sentry-go
Constantly, caw-caw-cawing
In raucous fidelity, always to live
With the shapes and shadows of their sombre wings.

Some think of them as sinister,
From the left-hand side of nature.
A hunted pheasant pleads in the arboreal dark.
How much I owe these birds, including crows,
As winter becomes spring, and grows, and grows.
And now it is raining on the stick nests.
This is their pale of settlement. I'll respect it.

Bluebottles

A black piece of winged innocence, commonly found irritating,
An anxious thought that needs to be smacked, dealt with,
Driven out, squashed, swatted with rolled headlines.
Some, though, don't mind them, and leave them alone
To their glassy entrapments, their frantic patrols
Up and down windows, their insect dementias.
For this bluebottle's body is rather beautiful,
Metallic but weightless energy, black with a blue shine,
One-hundred-per-cent committed to
Its singular identity, its life-without-options.
Little waster – if allowed to be – of fridges and larders,
Where do you sleep? Do you live long enough
To rest at night, and return in the morning
To your busy bluebottling endeavours? I could find out,
But I prefer to imagine you, tiny praetorians.
There was once a plague of you in my bookish office
Caused by a roast beef sandwich left below in the boiler room
By the engineer, where you bred and multiplied.
For weeks bluebottle cadavers kept reappearing
On books, and in books, like hallucinations
Punctuating scholarly print and Shakespeare's genius.
Your ancestry's infinite, your genealogy a mystery.
The Everyday Life of the Bluebottle – impossible!
So, spread your brittle wings, *Calliphora*.
Buzz off, dear blowfly, dine where you can,
And pester the cruel ones of mankind.

Garden Didactics

Mind measures itself as morning brightens.
From the hush of washed shrubs, a doomed pheasant
Rises in winged but flightless panic, its eye
Imprinted on my own, as if I'm one
Who'd flush it from its gardened hiding place
And end its fluster with a well-aimed gun.

Here, too, is what's left of a guzzled rabbit
Dined on by a lucky fox or buzzard,
Pecked now by crows. Dew steams from the grass.
Ground mist in the strath hides burn and hill.
If I light the heap of sneddins, leaves and branches,
How many mice and hedgehogs will I kill?

I watch the tiny, wicked wrens, the robins,
Blackbirds, thrushes, finches, a wren perched on
A camellia bud. A blue-grey, curious cat,
For whom all birds mean an instinctive bliss,
Compiles a rota of the nests he'll herrie,
A pretty, plump and purring Nemesis.

There's much to do, but not today I won't.
It's time to catch a bus and go to work,
Perform another kind of tending.
Is it different? – Owls, foxes, buzzards,
Those driven by instinctive selfishness,
Masters and mistresses of feline words.

Gardens are for wise ones, the long-in-the-tooth
Weed-pickers, opted out of push and 'spin'.
Here's where the worldly melts in earth and compost,
Wheel-barrowed weeds and watering can,
And where the work of man can be undone,
Though doing so's also the work of man.

An Actor Takes up Gardening

'Some men are born great, some achieve greatness,
And some have greatness thrust upon them' . . .
And some are born into the ranks of Rep
Or touring companies flogging second-rate
West End comedies in Hull and Harrogate,
Small parts on radio, a week-dead corpse
On *Morse*, and then five lines in flashback
To justify the fee more than the script.

A chunky whitewashed cottage in the Cotswolds
Eludes my wherewithal. It always will.
I don't complain. A flat in Milton Keynes
Suits me, and suits my barren economics.
Those forty-something, theatre-going chicks,
Who constitute, decidedly, my weakness,
Loathe my address. I strut upon a stage,
Which seems to mean I must be truly loaded.

And so, I took up gardening. Non sequitur?
Denying that discloses who I am,
Or who I have become, who pays his rent
Then spends what little's left on plants and shrubs,
Bulbs, seed, compost, spades, forks, rakes, hoes, pots, tubs.
Here I can contemplate a good review
And disregard the bad ones. My paradise,
Badgered by flight-paths and the growls of traffic,

Nurtures my 'Shakespeare Collection' – musk-rose,
Cowslip, primrose, woodbine and eglantine, thyme,
'Nodding violet', rosemary (remembrance
Those forty-something chicks don't feel for me),
Fennel, pansies (for 'thoughts'), Ophelia's plea
Recorded in her herbs and sweetheart flowers.
Frequently 'resting', I find it restful,
Almost as soothing as talking about it.

Roses soliloquise, and I grow old.
My agents called. Could I play Kent in *Lear*?
I've reached that age, and I'll audition for it.
Would forty-something ladies be enticed
By my old-man, avuncular sacrifice
As the benevolent Kent? I think they might.
God help me, but this could turn out the part
That recommends me to the public heart.

And rue. Don't forget rue. And marjoram,
Basil, parsley, chives, sage. Those sodding slugs
And snails die pissed or poisoned in my traps
Of sunken beer. Enough get through to dine
On my tender botany, the sticky swine.
Some claim we grow into a destined role
That's waiting for us, but we don't know which.
Is mine kindly old Kent? I don't feel like him.

The trouble is I look like what I do,
Part Donald Sinden, part gardening tosspot
Pontificating over leeks and lilies
In padded waistcoat and brown corduroys,
Green wellies, and showing off his trug
With sample runner beans, his ugly mug
Radiant with self-regard and ruddy tan,
Wielding a mean rake and meaner watering-can.

I could do that! But *Gardeners' World* refused
To speak to me. 'Drama for Schools' tomorrow.
Young hopefuls. Or hopelesses, more likely.
Still, it buys me gardening and pays the rent.
I'll play the martyred, hard-done-by Duke of Kent.
All actors, I suppose, must like being looked at,
Victims of inverted voyeurism. Our art
Means being other. We think we can outsmart

Identity and self. Thank God for gardens.
The solitude of toying with the earth.
The tiny dramas of recurrence. Dirt.
The daily management of green. Release
Into a realm of speechless, wordless peace.
Yes, I'll play Kent, if they should ask me to.
Right now I feel like Lear, as I rant through
This herbal wealth, suspiciously like dearth.

A Basket of Apples

in memory of Barbara Murray

I see them still as a painting by Peploe
Or even a lesser colourist on a good day,
These fruits of early autumn's visible taste.
A memory, but it's not one of sorrow.
Offered to all – 'Don't let them go to waste' –
Outside your office door, as if you'd said
'It's not all work, you know. Take a good bite.
Relish slowly.' That was your gift to us,
An annual present, freely given away,
Out of consideration, out of kindness.
Your country apples savoured of East Neuk light!
Apples, teaching, scholarship, and care –
Commonplace fruits, except you placed them there,
Their green, their gold, their yellow, bronze and red.

An Alternative Map of Scotland

A tramp I knew, a professional, long-distance
All-over-the-realm roamer of B-roads,
Slept in the long-cold kiln at Walkinshaw's
Abandoned brickworks. He showed me his map –
An outline map of Scotland, folded neatly,
And kept inside a dog-eared Robert Burns.
On it he'd plotted safe places, and the dates
He'd slept there. Where were the names of towns I knew?
Reality was in his balding head
Or unimportant. What he used was lore,
A secret geography, a handed-on
Knowledge of havens and hostels, the farms
Where he'd be sure of water, a day's work,
Privacy, and clean straw to bed down on.

I was with Sparrow Gray that July morning.
He was wearing his father's tin hat.
The bold Speug's legs were skinny and all knees.
I was wearing one of my uncle's pith helmets
With my Daddy's tin-hat slung over my shoulder.
In our khaki shorts, we could have looked like
Midget soldiers in the desert, hot for Rommel.
With his ex-Army rucksack, his gasmask bag,
The tramp looked like a snail, walking slowly
Towards the Barnsford Bridge. It was a map
Articulating poverty and movement,
Moving on, without momentum, a slow cruise
On worn boots, wearing most of his wardrobe.

We went inside the kiln once he was gone.
Dusty sunbeams shot through holes in its roof.
Speug held his nose. It didn't really stink.
The smell was old air, high temperatures
Of long ago trying to cool in the summer,
Maybe a scent of sleep, or whiff of dreams.
He'd left a note for the next occupant
Fixed to a nail in the wall. I took it down,
Went outside, read it, then put it back. It said,
'There's a good old soul in the first smallholding
Over the road, by the bridge. For sweeping,
And fixing a hinge on her outhouse door,
She gave me two boiled eggs, four buttered scones,
All the tomatoes I could pick and eat.'

Belfast to Edinburgh

for Michael and Edna Longley

At the beginning of descent, I see
Wind turbines cast their giant, spinning arms.
The Southern Uplands send out false alarms,
Semaphore shadows, all waving to me.

Then, still descending, as the windows weep
Or something out beyond the tilted wing
Surrenders to the planet's suffering,
Plural phenomena that never sleep,

A far-off brightness shines on the wet plane.
A cockpit voice says something about doors.
The Forth Bridge is a queue of dinosaurs.

A field of poppies greets a shower of rain.

Robert Fergusson

To wander through these frosted leaves,
Scuffing, kicking, deceives
No one in the drift of days.
I feel the cold erase
Part of my life, as my shoes sift
Dead leaves for a dead gift,
For that lost thing. I play the sleuth
Searching for health, or youth.
Something about a coat is lonely,
'As if . . .', 'If only . . .'

A V of geese has cracked the sky.
You would have seen them fly
Across St Andrews, Eden, Tay.
Those eighteenth-century
Fergussonian geese. Those feathered
Long-necked icons of instinct, weathered
Beyond endurance, fit
Too neatly into it,
This picture of madness, art,
Delighting the voice, breaking the heart.

High spirits, then the low, so low
You don't know where to go,
Or look, or say, or what to do
While the elusive clue
Stays secret in the rotting leaves,
Little land-star, the light that grieves

For human suffering
And the hope it can bring
Just by looking, turning
Leaves with a foot, the mind burning . . .

Another flight of geese goes by
With its communal cry.
Something about a shoe is lonely . . .
'As if . . .', 'If only . . .'
Such are the icons of the daft.
The dog sang, and the cat laughed,
And the cow jumped over the moon.
A half-remembered tune
Or half-forgotten song –
'What's wrong? What's wrong? What's wrong?'

Lyric oblivion. Earth-star,
I scuff for you. You are
Almost visible, like a cure,
Or lost, remembered thing, the lure
That leads me on, and through
Leathery chestnuts, and the blue
Frost-bitten sycamores.
Those who die mad, at twenty-four's
Promise of future, sing
For ever of their suffering.

I'm getting closer to you, working
My way to where you're lurking.
Under this pile? Here? There?
I scuff and sift them both. There? Where?

I can't go on like this.
Lovely woman, give me your kiss.
Robert, I hear your howl
In the ungraduated owl
Who sits so wisely on my summer-house,
His prey already posthumous.

The winded leaves give up
Their multitude of ghosts
And huddle into wetness.
Do you hear? I've ceased to rhyme.
What good did it do you, keeping time,
Beat after neoclassical beat?
You wrote little of love . . .
You shouldn't have gone to Edinburgh.
I've made a fire in the rain
To keep the crow away.

It stalks my dreams, and barks
Before breakfast, a patriarch's
Command, and my coffee cup
Shakingly lifted up.
Too much Enlightenment brings forth
Snoring Reason. For what it's worth,
You should have stayed in Fife,
Or the Mearns, or taken a wife.
Something about paper is lonely . . .
'As if . . .', 'If only . . .'

Bewigged by candlelight among
Auld Reekie's massed, unsung
Choristers of nibbed law,
You must have heard the caw

Croak in your mind, the ink-black rook
That perched on your half-written book.
By drafted candlelight
In tenemented night
You would have heard your first
Bird-whispers of the accursed –

Rough laughter from a distant close,
The way sounds, too, metamorphose
To audible shadows
Passing across windows
On the warlock wind. Ah, what ghosts
Blow in across our eastern coasts,
Whisky and syphilis
Each with its toxic kiss –
Visionary, vernacular,
The brain's beacon, the earth-star.

Give me time to find my mind
Then give me time to lose it

It's a condition of verse
That it should make life worse.
Run with the fox and box with the hare,
Whatever I do is a robin's prayer
And speaks my mind to feathered God
For I'm one of an awkward squad
Who lives with the song thrush
In its dacha, in the hush
Between the road and evening
In the tree-swish when birds sing.

Night-Walk

Wind shook the winter trees on that dark night.
I'd walked too far, without a single light
To be seen from the low, dark, sheltered dip
On the old road, forcing night-scholarship
On me, a trick of eyes in the pitch black
Moonlessness, starlessness, the puddled track
Deeper than I remembered. To stand still there
Meant breathing ink-black mediaeval air,
As if in a woodcut. I'd strayed beyond
Distance, stayed out too long. On awkward ground,
I found my confidence was a lot less than
The footsure instinct of a local man.
By gurgling unseen ditches, I could take
Rough bearings, knowing where I was, and ache
For my dinner and such. Instead I chose –
Or did I choose? – a daft nocturnal pose.
I stood still in the hope I'd understand
Mysteries of that wooded bottomland,
Ivied oaks by the torrent, and taller trees
Beyond them, higher up, and the black space
Between them. Nothing visible. Walking
By touch of walking stick, and by talking
To myself . . . Whispered notations of wet ground
Surrounded by the waters' watery sound
Turned up their volume as I neared the bridge
They buffeted against, the force and surge
Of streams in spate. But still, not quite enough
To budge the eighteenth century's repaired, rough
Stonework, or force its humpbacked nature from

Its root in time, its ancestral home
Cemented deeply into local rocks'
Stone-measurements within our mantled clocks.

Down in that carved hollow, diminished wind
Uttered its sheltered presence, disciplined
By slopes. It felt like damp fur on my cheek,
Half-active moistness, half-still, non-specific
Animal silk. I felt historyless,
Free, frightened, independent, raw. Solace
From rural and nocturnal solitude
Seeped into me, and creakings in the wood
Made themselves heard above the steady spate's
Hectoring eloquence, repeated threats
Sneering like bully-boys. With my stout stick,
I tapped forward. What's the word? Scotopic –
A Scot who can't see in the dark! Rain fell.
The darkness tightened. Night was mineral.
I took a battering by the parapet
On the budgeless bridge. I heard it groan and fret.
The night had put its shoulder to a door
That murderers tried to force in sung folklore
And balladry.

– *Mary Beaton, and Mary Seaton, and Mary Carmichael*
   and me!

                    A night-soaked antiquarian!
A night not to be out but to be in in . . .
But local, Pierian. My Muse's sky-wells, rain,
Winter's invisible roses, the sovereign
Permanent storm, that drops to claw the ground
And sniff and scavenge like a hungry hound,

While in the treetops, breaking branches, it
Ushered the wilds of weather to their limit –
A *good* night to be out in. I hold fast
To the native, the present-in-the-past,
Past-in-the-present, to the pre-Christian,
Pre-Reformation and pre-Presbyterian.

In the foundry of blood there is nothing
Ethical – it is what land and weathering
Tell the big place of here, and where I stood
In solitude surpassing solitude,
A keeper of a fragile bridge or gate
Protecting time, with peace to contemplate
Its datelessness. From daylight memory,
I knew of ivied trees, wild raspberry
Thick by the banks, perfervid botany
Of which the wind and night made ebony,
Winged and invisible but somehow there
In the twig-fragments in the howling air.
There was nocturnal substance to it, earth,
Water, air, absence of light and fire, dearth
Of them, like a remembered rarity.
Immeasurable darkness. I felt no pity,
No kindness in it, neither tenderness
Nor comfort in its slaps and angry kiss.

Night like a terror chronicle, I thought,
Walking blindly, footnote after footnote
In a Pictavian night-storm where the wind
Blew from the northeast like a gale imagined
Rather than matter-of-fact, a tempest
Brimming with ancient torments, each fierce gust

A scud of horror, squeaks and groans of trees
The cries of children, women, on their knees
Before the Vikings or English soldiery,
The worst of time, the worst of history
Proclaimed in naked weather. Easier ground,
Freed from the woodland, proved me homeward bound.
I suffered time, then closed my door on it,
Sat in the dark, and sipped the infinite,
Hearing the lashing wind cry out my name
And the hammering rain my pride and shame.

The House of the Blind

When you sat on the upper deck of the bus
You could see the white metal banisters
On the stepped pathways.

Once, on a winter's morning,
I saw someone being taught to climb steps.
The rail would have been cold and wet on his hands.

That spring, a raincoated man in dark spectacles
Would have felt similar cold and wet,
But been refreshed by the scent of lilacs.

On a summer's day, I saw a woman
Instructed in the use of her first guide dog.
Even now the tug on her arm pulls at my heart.

I could be the last poet in the language
To say 'heart' in the traditional way.
I hope not. I'm writing about eyes.

After a catastrophe of spectacles,
This autumn I walk in a blur.
My daughter's nudge on my arm makes me think of
    that stranger.

The coffee was good. I was on my third cup.
From opened windows across the street
Instrumentalists were practising –

Flutes, clarinets, trumpets, violins, several pianos.
In lulls for tuition or advice, a fine soprano
Stopped people in their shoes, listening.

A cellist surrendered to Bach with a passion.
I could imagine the genderless sway,
Planing the air, ironing sound.

I felt so glad to be in Prague, and free,
With time on my hands, and *Turandot* in the evening.
An oboe lingered, in love with Mozart.

Several students emerged with cased instruments.
They unpocketed, then unfolded, their white sticks.
I think the waiter was watching for my reaction.

His smile was benign, but proud, and defiant.
All day, every day, he listens to their music.
His smile broadened, and he nodded,

Approving my look of sympathetic surprise;
And, after three shots of strong black coffee, my cup
Was the more tremblingly lifted up.

III

After Louis Braille accidentally put his eye out
With an awl in his father's workshop,
And the other eye sympathised with its dead partner,

A great kindness began in his darkness.
There was reading by raised dots before him,
Invented for French artillerymen to plan

The fall of shot in the dark without giveaway lamps.
The gunners couldn't read, not even in daylight.
Braille refined, perfected, and made a useful thing.

Thomas Edison invented the gramophone
To provide speaking books for the blind –
Tin Pan Alley and the entire repertoire

Recorded from a foundation in benevolence.
I've watched a blind student read a poem in Braille,
And then say it aloud, in perfect cadence,

Her voice delighting me. She's never seen
A poem, but she reads and hears. I write
To be read by eyes, and mind, and fingers.

IV

When you lose an eye, then you can lose the other,
Like Louis Braille, by 'sympathetic ophthalmia'.
It doesn't happen often. But you lose a dimension,

As my love discovered, hanging out the washing
On a line that felt uncertain, flat, and vague.
After that, I did it. Sympathy's mutual.

I hung the washing on a line that wavered.
That was as nothing to my love's nightmare –
Hanging washing on a line that wasn't there.

The Monocle of Professor J. Norton-Smith

In that grey, black-flecked tweed suit of yours,
A monocle looked almost appropriate –
A portliness of eye that matched the waistcoat
And went with your moustache and pukka voice.

Today I broke a magnifying glass
And the fallen lens reminded me of you
Playing the banjo in a three-piece suit,
Wearing a monocle, and playing well,

Astonishing the ghosts of New Orleans.
A mediaevalist from Philadelphia,
You snorted snuff like an outdated laird.
Your skin was thick as fourteenth-century vellum,

But it wasn't nearly thick enough.
I remember being driven across the Tay Bridge
In your Jaguar automatic, talking about
The Kingis Quair, which you'd just edited,

Ignoring the traffic, a perfect Mr Toad;
And your record collection, all 78s
That you played on an ancient gramophone.
You had the style of your first editions,

A merry manner with a bottle of malt;
You cooked a breakfast like nobody else.
Scholar, perfectionist, your snobbishness
Felt more like fun to me than fault.

I consult my ostentatious pocket watch
As if reading my autobiography.
Is it that time already? Years go by.
Friends suffer, then they die. I've known

A 'character' or ten in my lifetime;
Of any one it would be true to say,
'There'll never be another you.'
I keep them in the locket of a rhyme.

Near Myths

Pollution, or a clever stunt pulled off
By wintry sunset, or my bad eyesight,
But here's some stuff you didn't have much time for.
Or were you kidding me, prince of irony? –
A serious frost, a blackbird on the shed,
Frozen glass silvering a greenhouse,
An inky dusk in cloudy North East Fife,
Bucolic winter twilight in the north
(Celtic, Rangers, Hibs, Hearts, Raith Rovers)
Ice-stiffened ivy, trees I need to prune
And shrubs turned shabby by the fading day
(St Mirren, Aberdeen, Dundee United).
29th of December, and I've just heard you're dead.

Old friend, you're gone, and gone for ever.
For what it's worth, I'll sit out here tonight
As soon as it's warmed up enough
In my Zhivago hut, nursing arthritis
With whisky, notebook, pen, and ink,
Wearing my Churchillian boilersuit, thermals,
A yellow muffler, and writing with gloves on,
A heater crackling with electric dust.
'Oh yes,' you'd say. 'A sentimental berk.'

I remember football in that muddy park
And how you dribbled in a semi-dark
Much like this one, same time of year,
As if into yourself, then wandered off
With the ball at your feet, a one-man Spurs.

Your myth was London's multi-thousand streets,
An A to Z of love and its addresses,
Plus restaurants, offices, black cabs swarming
On Charing Cross Road. You could hail a cab
With expertise that seemed like telepathy
And get me to Kings Cross and the train for home.
Why did waiters always come to your nod,
The slightest flick of your raised eyebrows?

That's what I miss. Your worldly skill, contempt,
Your withering wisdom, tenderness, concern,
Your sanity that could unbalance others' –
Plugging the point, relentless, reasonable,
Our man of clearest mind, our perfect critic.

I trumped your teasing by teasing you back,
You loveable bastard. How two grown men,
Both heterosexual by profound conviction,
Could tease each other so beats me.
I don't know, I just don't know
Any longer why friends treat each other so
To teasing and sparring. So long ago;
And yet it seems it happened yesterday.

Blame me. Shame me. I am worthy of both.
You, too, old friend? Now that you're gone,
Can I speak to you plainly? I'll be speaking
With you, old friend, for ever and anon,
Remembering the Pillars, Bailey's Bistro,
And yet another emptied house carafe
Quaffed as if we couldn't get enough
To oil the 'miraculous school of poetry',
Those afternoons in the covert Capricorn.

I raise my gloved glass to memorialise
Contemplated Alka-Seltzers, a morning dram
Downed in a oner at 11 a.m.
In Westbourne Terrace, Dorset Square, Wimbledon,
Or in a shady bar in shady Soho.

Provence

Strange, that I loved the smell of it
    But didn't know its name.
        Neither did you –
Green, aromatic spell of it
Casting its herbal fennel-fame
    Over the warm hillside
    And its steaming dew.
And there was me, and there was you
    In the fair grass-tide.

That morning on the Luberon
    Cézanne was love and truth
    And so were we
Basking in that September in
The last years of our coupled youth
    On the warm hillside
    And its steaming dew.
And there was me, and there was you
    In the fair grass-tide.

Art, Poetry, and Love, were stays
    In post-Impressionist light
    And time was gone
Wandering through September days
Towards the autumn and the night
    On that warm hillside
    And its steaming dew.
And there was me, and there was you
    In the fair grass-tide.

Self-Portraits

(Rembrandt)

Aged thirty-four, his headgear has a touch of style,
With its gold chain, or gold-thread filigree;
But in the partner piece, aged sixty-three,
His hat, though confident, deliberates
A contrast – almost, but not yet, senile.
A simple narrative, it innovates
As only truth can, setting his life free
In its discoveries of age, unflattered
By his glass, those art-worn eyes, booze-battered
Big Dutch hooter, and the famous moustache,
A tuft of hair beneath his bottom lip.
A careful, barbered man, his draughtsmanship
Served honesty with artistry's panache.

Aged sixty-three, he clasps his hands as if in prayer.
His younger self leans on a balcony,
His hands half-secret but in harmony
With his bright eyes, as if to prove his art
Depends on them, while grey, receding hair
In later years shows an experienced heart,
Wisdom with-and-without the irony
That makes life bearable and stares into
Non-narcissistic mirrors of the true.
Less ostentatious now, more prosperous
Than ever, coated finely, darker shadows
Prove the autumnal, while just one thumb shows
Anxiety, a gesture without fuss.

Secure, as if he has outlived desire's distress
Or need of hope . . . The well-examined life!
All the tricks of his trade, brush, palette knife,
Pigments, charcoal, directed at his face
In a mirror where private truths confess
Their secrets, pride, security, disgrace
Reflected in the strangely absent wife.
Harder to do in words? So I suppose.
I cannot draw myself in verse or prose,
While I use mirrors only to tie my tie,
Shave cheeks, and comb my hair, don't even own
A full-length glass, that visual microphone
That ups the volume on the macro-eye.

How do you write about yourself? How do you say,
'I do not like the way I have become,'
And not feel stupid? Muses, strike me dumb
Should I avoid a necessary truth
And compromise my hoarded artistry.
Something about ageing makes me witness youth
Surviving in me like a troublesome
Dilemma. Rembrandt saw two men (at least)
And so do I. One's young, an arriviste;
The other's older and ambitionless.
But still, I couldn't show my punctured nose
Or to a mirror strike a thoughtful pose.
Eye kissing eye is an internal kiss –

Not in my temperament. That two arts differ so!
Music's another matter. Substance of sound
Means substance of oblivion, a bond
Created by how what you're listening to
Links to the sights and thoughts you cannot know
Are those composers meant to be the true
Impressions of a reverie, spellbound
In the bubble of self. Ach, what is art
If not recurrences eyes, ears, and heart
Renew, refresh, over and over, time
And time again, probing the sensory
And ethical, in search of a story
Pulling together colour, form, love, rhyme?

The body and its mind, the sentient intellect,
Go rooting like pigs' snouts for shape and form
Where self encounters the eccentric norm
Known as humanity – grey, overweight,
The body jiggered, bloated, stiff, and wrecked
By appetites or worse. It's wearing late.
He holds his hands, either to keep them warm
Or understate the artistry and skill
With which he worked – instinctive, physical –
And then puts down his brush to walk away
And leave himself for ever frozen in
Timeless silence and his own reflection
Caught in the seasons of eternity.

Refrigerated garden darkness. I tread frost.
Footsteps of solitude. The loneliest road
Leads sixty paces west to the all-hallowed
Night-view of a hillside, windless and cold,
A perfect night in which to count the cost
Of what I've done, or did not. Growing old.
Weeds, prunings, waste, barrow-by-barrowload,
I've wheeled and pushed until my aching back
Begged me to pack it in and hit the sack.
Now, though, on Boxing Day, at 1 a.m.,
I supervise the night, and see my truth –
Rembrandt's ambitious age, ambitious youth –
And know myself at last for who I am.

How to Write Verse without Anyone Knowing

I owned a crystal inkwell with a silver lid,
But kept no ink in it, or none that you could see.
It perplexed my father, watching me write in invisible ink
On paper he brought from the tyre factory
Rolled in a pocket of his navy blue overalls
Worn over his sub-managerial navy blue suit.
'Why do you need paper?' he asked, much puzzled
By my twelve-year-old's trance-like concentration.
'No one else can see it,' I said, snapping out of it. 'But I can.'

When I took to listening to opera on the wireless,
He said, 'I can tell Italian when I hear it,
But I didn't know you could. How do you follow the story?'
'Easy-peasy,' I said, the perfect prig that I was then.
'I've read all the opera stories in a book in the library.'
'God help us, but you know all the answers,' he said.
'No, I don't know them all. I just know where to find them.'
'"One Fine Day",' my mother said. 'My favourite. *Madame
    Butterfly.*'

Fragility

What asks me to walk out tonight
If not the honeysuckle's scent
Or thinking of that frantic cabbage-white
And wondering where on earth, or air, it went?

It fluttered off a buddleia cone
After a heavy shower released,
Somehow, so many in just one, just one
Puff of wings in the buzzing bee-policed

Outburst of windy semi-sunshine
When robins, finches, wrens, and tits
Flew to the feeders, instinctive and benign,
Mounting their famished, beaky visits.

I listen to my old watch tick
Against the smell of earth and shrubs,
Then find my bench, tapping my walking-stick
Between the roses in their fragrant tubs.

And how like most of life this is,
Existence, its serenity,
Aware of time keeping its promises,
Facing what happens without self-pity.

Bon Voyage

for Marco Fazzini

I arrived in the city where the streets have no names
As if there were never hero statesmen or soldiers,
No victories or public anniversaries or saints.
Nor are there numbers or letters. You find where you are
By landmarks – bridges, churches, theatres, squares
With monuments to the Unknown Plumber, the Baker,
The Fishmonger, and so on through traditional trades.
People know where they're going when they've arrived,
By familiar faces. You can sniff where you are,
Once you know how, by bakeries, tanneries, print shops,
Potteries, coffee blenders, breweries, wine merchants,
Or routes plotted from the famous opera house.
(God knows how post gets delivered, but it does.)
There are no hotels. Tourism is not forbidden,
Merely discouraged. 'Let others sleep elsewhere'
Seems close to the city's unofficial motto.
'They should learn that we who live here are superior.'
Taxis, therefore, are non-existent, like trams, or buses,
Postcards, souvenirs, or political parties
Where it's a case of 'Vote for me, if you can be bothered'.
National or foreign news eludes the newspaper
(There's only one) which is dedicated to gossip,
Reports of dog-fouling, sexual scandal, and advertisements.
The national government has given up on this city,
Only too willing to leave it to eccentricity,
Somewhere beyond taxation and conscription,
An invisible city not worth the trouble.
(Already, the railway station seemed far away.

My suitcase weighed like a cruiser's anchor.)
Two hundred paces west of the big basilica
Subtle changes in the local dialect can be heard
Quite clearly by a studious or attentive ear.
There are as many dialects as districts.
I'd asked my friend, the last time I saw him,
In Scotland, how on earth I'd find his apartment.
He'd smiled and said, 'Use your *telefonino*.
Just describe what's around you. It'll be a matter
Of a few right turns, a few lefts and straight-aheads.
No one ever gets completely lost.
On one corner of my street, there's a butcher,
On the other, across the road, a patisserie.
It's the only such configuration in the city.
I'd meet you at the station, but I think it best
That you find your own way, and learn our mysteries.'
So I was homed in by rights, lefts, and doglegs,
By trials and errors, one stupidity
After another, several hot piazzas, four bridges,
A couple of cold beers in somnolent cafés
Watched by the drowsily suspicious drinkers
Sipping their local colourful concoctions.
And my friend was growing increasingly ratty.
'Your sense of direction is that of a cretin.
What is the idiom? Pull your socks down!'
A smell of fish wafted from the wharves.
'Do you know a street,' I asked a stranger,
'A butcher on one corner, a patisserie opposite?'
It was at what they call the hour of moth-light.
'Of course, it's unique in the entire city.
Come, I'll show you.' I noticed that his smile
Echoed my friend's exactly, the very same

Sardonic glow, meaning that he possessed
Savoir faire, that I didn't, and never would.
Children were playing games in the dusty dusk,
Skipping ropes for girls, tops and hoops for boys.
Two bridges later, one piazza, some lefts and rights,
And I dialled my friend. 'Thank God. At last. I'm famished.
Three flights up, and it's the green door on the left.'

Class Photograph

Renfrew High School, 1956

We were Elizabethan girls and boys,
Too young for politics, too old for toys.
Then Hungary and Suez changed all that,
Or so it feels in tired old retrospect.
Nostalgia corrodes the intellect.
It makes you want to eat your coat and hat.

One foot in childhood, one in adolescence,
Rock Around the Clock made far more sense
Even than *The Battle of the River Plate* –
Stiff upper lips and Royal Navy dash,
Its Technicoloured brio and panache
Heroic, goreless, brilliant, out of date.

Like Ovaltineys in their Start-rite shoes –
It catches up on you, it really does,
This looking back, this old class photograph.
Be-blazered in our uniforms and ties
(*Who he? Who she?*) – pensioners in disguise
As who they were, a pictured epitaph.

Pillar-boxes still red (though not much else is)
And the scarcely visible orthodoxies
All still in place, plus global urgency,
Destructive wars abroad . . . And yet, God bless
Democracy, dissent, and the NHS
Which underpins our civic decency.

At Lake Balaton

We're told the villa was a rendezvous
For summer Habsburgs. countesses, archdukes,
Austro-Hungarian gentry, their children, servants –
They're easily imagined on the lawns,
Tennis courts, in little yachts, coy swimming costumes,
White-trousered men strolling the stony beach,
Parasolled women, or an imperial angler,
A couple watching a flight of fine swans.

A hotel now (of course) we're told it was
Where, until 1989, ministers,
Party officials, or pampered dignitaries
Rested, caroused, conspired, or took their ease
By highest invitation. Swans still flew,
Or floated on the lake, and birds still sang.
Boats and yachts still sauntered on the water.
A watery wind still whispered in the trees.

We discuss poetry, the translation of your own
Language into itself, and translation
From your own language into another.
For all I know, the Habsburgs talked about
Poetry incessantly, or Communists,
Or Admiral Horthy. Don't talk about the war!
We talk about Miklós Radnóti, his
'Letter to My Wife'. The fat beer-swilling lout

That is History passes across my mind
In sweaty vapour at a snail's speed, leaving
A snail's sticky path laden with data
For other snails, for me, too, and for you,
And you, for everyone. It's a strange house
That doesn't outlive its inhabitants, who
And what they were. Is it make-believe to make up?
Is it feigning? Or, the more made up, more true?

I imagine fragrant ball-gowned ladies
Descending a staircase in 1913
On uniformed arms. I would, though, wouldn't I?
I'm fond of ball-gowned ladies, and of fragrance.
Not fond, though, of aristocratic antics,
Imperial protocol, and uniforms.
I love a lovely arm in a long black glove.
That's not a fetish. It's just common sense.

Not that I know enough about it all –
But that's my way with almost everything.
I dream myself into Communist years
In Hungary, and Balaton, and here.
I see the grim politicos, and their wives,
Sure of themselves, and of posterity,
In the aftermath of 1956,
Relaxing, soaking up the atmosphere,

A sanatorium where pride and power
Unwind in sunshine, whatever the politics.
It's a beautiful place, guarded, remote,
As all such places are – the house behind

Dense trees, discreet, off-putting guarded gate.
All countries have them – the powerful's retreat,
A place to be human in, where crimes dissolve
In the forgetfulness of pleasured mind.

Radnóti died on a forced march from Serbia.
By something like a miracle, his poem
Survived the bullets and the grave. It lives.
Domestic redemption – his love survives;
It breathes in this and every other air,
Timeless, beyond oblivion. Take heart,
My friends. We're not forgotten. Nor is he.
Like a night-cry, he has entered our lives,

Even in this house, where layered memories
Patrol the corridors, the mini-bars,
Beds, desks, chairs, wardrobes, mirrors, sinks and baths,
The terrace where we meet to talk and drink.
It's all so elegant, and very charming.
Religious tranquillity, the calm lake –
Do we deserve this hush of landlocked waves,
This seriousness, in which we meet to think

Together, polyglot, with poetry,
Not politics, the raw phenomenon
We share? I lie awake and think about
A wicked century, and of a man,
A poet, and his wife, who somehow save us
From what happened, a little token of
Redemptive love, and what they gave us
Means we should try to live as best we can.

And love and write as best we can, before
Monstrous and unexpected circumstance
Shuts us up for ever. I cast my thoughts wide.
A linen-suited lepidopterist
Enters my fancy. He is also a prince
Freed from the desks of state for a fortnight
To spend his leisure with a net, chasing
Butterflies in the reed beds and the forest.

His evening passes listening to Liszt.
Imagination flashes backwards to
A woman in the Thirties, playing the piano.
Wife to a right-wing, near-Fascist minister,
She's rediscovered love in her husband.
That prince, now very old, listens to her,
Except he's young, and listening in the past,
Enamoured of Liszt, or art, or else of her.

She, too, grows old, and dies, as the prince does,
As we will too. Past, present, and future –
They coexist in an imagination.
It's through the folds of time we find the truth,
Or so we think, or dream ourselves into
Its multi-mysteries. Aristocrat,
Fascist, Communist . . . But what's the category
Describes *our* party? A studious sleuth

Decades from now could sniff another layer
In the heaped time of here. Late Capitalist? –
How do you free yourself from history?
What sheer inventiveness creates a space

For who a person is, what he/she does?
The greater freedom is one unachieved
By governments and ideologies
Or economics and the marketplace.

Radnóti, disinterred, identified
By your poems, freed from earth's forgetfulness,
You are anchored in Europe. Holocaust
Victim, rotted icon, disintegrated poet,
Husband, I've heard your voice, and now
Embrace our European sorrow in
Your story. Your poetry is your ghost.
I've lived, but I don't know the half of it.

I've sensed your strangeness in a marbled room.
Scholar of sorrow, and a history-worrier,
What's this remorseful anger gnaws at me
Again, and leads me to rehearse, rehearse,
Again, and again, a terrible century?
Why can't I just put it away and forget?
Poetic memory's the world's worst curse
And it contaminates my awkward verse.

Lake Balaton's nocturnal shimmer, lights
On the far shore, the whisper of reed beds –
My nationality's dismantled by
Tideless waters. Astral reflections skim
Across the darkness. What people choose to do
In their liberty, in their own time, is all.
It is good to be free and responsible.
And Gabriella takes her midnight swim.

Blue Day

Rising at 6 a.m. in winter is
To greet beginnings at their terminus.
I get up in the dark and then come home
To a nocturnal, rural semi-slum
In the dark sticks beside a main road –
The short days' daily, dismal episode.
I spoke to a stranger, then read a thriller.
I sipped a dram made by a fine distiller,
Then phoned my mother, then I combed my hair,
Without a mirror, sitting in my chair
Before a notebook at my littered desk.
I could be debonair
Instead of an ampersand or asterisk.
Time for exuberance – *Whoo! Whoo!*
'Night Train', 'Chattanooga Choo Choo',
'Atchison, Topeka and Santa Fe',
'A Train', and I take it away
With stiff Martinis in the dining-car
For Daphne, Josephine and Sugar Kane,
And, ladies, we are runnin' wild
Where laughs are laughed and smiles are smiled.
So, Wednesday, don't fence me in,
And then I'll play you 'All the Things You Are'
On my old battered clarinet
That isn't quite exhausted yet,
And play you 'In a Mellotone'
On my spit-watered beat-up tenor saxophone,
And then I'll give you – well, just maybe –
Tragic Marilyn's 'My Melancholy Baby'.

English (a Scottish Essay)

I didn't choose you, nor did you choose me.
I was born into a version called Accent.
I haven't lost it, nor could it lose me –
I own it; it owns me, with my consent.
Some of my words were Playground. Others, though,
Came straight from an indigenous long ago
Out of old mouths in sculleries, or learned
Hanging around byres. Spoken, unwritten nouns,
Strong verbs, swept out of classrooms, overturned
Their fingerwagging mockery and frowns –
'*Speak properly!*' A 'Scottish education' –
Groomed to profess complexities of nation
In an amended tongue, while writing verse
In ancient cadences and noise, my voice
A site of rebel mimicry, its burrs,
Slurs, Rs, its sly, involuntary 'choice'.
    The wireless gave me safety, bield and space
To fill my room with music's commonplace
Sound for itself, not meaning. Moving dials
Across jazz and concertos, I cleared off
From the parish across a neutral aerial's
Invisible bridge. I couldn't get enough
Meaningless babble's radio-polyglot
Valve-busting links to Rome and Camelot.
Arthurian radio! Imagination!
Through knob-turned atlases of noise I found
Another and unfathomable nation
So overheard that it was underground.
Radio Inchinnan! Radio Renfrew!

Can you still hear me? Am I getting through?
That nation's called Poetry. It's policed
By Muses, not by critics, theorists, nor
Chief Constables hyping a long-deceased
National Bard as the forevermore
'Authentic' measure of the way to write
Poetry grounded in archaic hindsight
And retrospective fame, the Robert Burns
Syndrome. – 'Just write like him, and you'll be true
To Scotland when its good old self returns.
Then you'll be true to us, and true to you.'
Why do I disbelieve it? Why do I feel
It harms both mine and Burns's commonweal?
Because I do? Is it instinctive only
To think and feel the language I write in
Selects me to be snapped at, and feel lonely
When it's the tongue I know, that I delight in?
English I'm not. As language, though, you're mine,
Disinterested, Scots, also benign,
Or so I try to make you, keeping time
On beats of Burns and Shakespeare, Pope and Frost,
Plundered affinities, rhythm and rhyme
From any place or time and intercrossed,
MacCaig with Milton, Stevenson with Keats,
Byron, Browning, scanning the nationless beats.
    Not nationality but language. So,
What's odd or treacherous other than the name?
Not that I like the name – all my bon mots
In somewhere else's tongue! Why scourge and blame
History for what had to happen in it
When you can't cancel it, not by a minute,
Not by a year, never mind an epoch?

Go back, reclaim the past, to when we spoke
Each one of us as quintessential Jock?
Where, when, was that? Who were these purer folk
Whose tongues absolved them from an 'English' stain
And wrote their poetry in a native grain
So aboriginal its recited truth
Sang nation and confirmed a State from one
Infatuated lyrical in-love mouth,
A great God-help-us not-to-be-outdone
Embrace of who the Scots are, or might be,
Massive mouthpiece of *national* poetry?
No one – thank God! For we've got three sound tongues
In which to utter poetry, and three
Good reasons, therefore, for our native songs
To triplicate our nationality.
My Muse is mine alone; but still, she's free
To join her sisters in their choir of three,
If she should want to, and, if she should not,
She'll get her dander up if you accuse
My Lady she's an insufficient Scot –
She's not a politician, she's a Muse!
That sacred girl insists work be exact,
True to the spirit, measure, and the fact.
  What happened happened, though – 1707,
To go no farther back than that loud date.
Half understood, denied, or unforgiven,
It's not my number and it's not my fate.
The past's an interesting cadaver;
But let it rot. Don't let it stink for ever
Somewhere at the foot of the garden, or,
Worse, in your head. *Get that skull out of here!*
Rip all old pages off the calendar!
Try cranium-scrape, but get your head in gear!

– A memo to myself, to fight the ghost
Who steps from disappointment and distrust.
I've seen him sleeping on the 95,
Tricorned, peruked, an eighteenth-century gent,
Grave-robbed but looking very much alive,
A fierce old cove of the Enlightenment.
Damn *Braveheart*. It's the mind, not pikes and swords
Or martyred schiltrons but well-chosen words
Turn time around, direct it on ahead
Instead of back to where the clocks are stopped,
Stopwatches held in the hands of the dead.
When backs were stabbed and the secrets shopped,
Whisperers served the cause of trade. – A spit,
A wink, a shake of hands, and that was it.
Signed, sealed, delivered, to themselves, to them,
To us – Great Britain, that convenient phrase,
Rhotistic, tri-syllabic nasty poem
Invented by a Treaty, tuned to praise
Union, aggrandisement, possession, money,
An archipelago of gluttony.
    Lists of neurotic Scotticisms; earnest
Desires to write and speak like Englishmen;
A wilful limpness in the national wrist –
Heyday of Edinburgh elocution!
But on the streets and closes Scotticisms
Meant nothing to apprentices and besoms.
Law Lords and luminaries spoke Braid Scots
Although when such as Kames sat down to write
Memorials or aesthetics, subtle thoughts
Found their expression in an erudite
Capital-city eighteenth-century prose
As natural to him as his daily brose.
Braid Scots was proseless in Lord Kames's time.

Abundant prose there was, but not in Scots –
Although not pre-prose, Scots prefers to rhyme,
Foxed by the plots and counterplots
Of history – 1603, 1707,
Those dates by which our languages are driven.
Ramsay, Ross, Fergusson, and balladeers
Wrote their full-throated oppositional poems
For native minds and aboriginal ears
To reassert the sound of vocal home's
Domestic noise, the tongue of a *patrie*
Wagging and singing, almost a refugee
In the mouths of its speakers, and pathos
Beginning, the sorrow of movement, shifts
In time as change became perceived as loss
And what came in instead felt less than gifts
Between tongue and teeth, but as something fake.
A foreign language for men on the make
In London or Calcutta, Hudson's Bay,
British regiments, enslaved plantations,
Or on the London stage in 'the Scottish play',
Banks and Westminster, the British nation's
Class-lingo infiltrated 'social stations' –
Legged up by legover. Intimate unions
Ran parallel before the paper Act
In Anglo-Scottish sexual communions
Where love and love of property, the fact
Embedded snugly in commercial chance,
Led straight to land, preferment, and finance.
    Historical amusement, not treachery
In that careerist scramble, changing tongues
With the polished skills of sonic forgery
And climbing up the social ladder's rungs
By each perfected step of mouth – 'station'

Determined by 'correct' pronunciation!
As well forget or turn a blind eye on
Ancestral roguery, so far back it's
A shoulder diehard dreaming Tories cry on.
Best, though, to know your past, then call it quits,
For if you don't you'll Balkanise your brain
Or Irish it with history's inhumane
Serbianisms, ethnic cleansing's dire
Epic revenges for events before –
Hundreds of years before – present desire
And possible fulfilment. MacMinotaur
Lurks in this labyrinth, sectarian,
Preening his tammy, polishing his grin.
  Haar settles on the mist-dimmed coast of Fife.
St Andrews Castle's introverted stone
Withdraws into its tended afterlife.
July's inertia's a Scotophone
Sensation as I wander round the walls
All ears for ghost-words, listening to my pulse
Tapping to blood's stone history as speech,
Knox and Fife's local lairds, in English pay,
Defending this, Knox taking time to preach
Despite the shot of French artillery.
An archaeologist of wrathful breath,
I recreate his accent, tongue and teeth,
But it's all in my head. Nobody knows
How Knox (or Shakespeare) spoke, just that they did,
And wrote. It's all a scholarly suppose
To think old writers sound the way they read.
Knox, though, the firebrand, rasping faith and Hell,
Clichéd the Presbyterian decibel
With pulpit rhetoric and prolix soul
Fuelled by his brawny days pulling an oar,

Singing a Reformation barcarolle
As a French galley-slave, plotting his roar,
Scotland's future, and a Bibleless tongue –
Pulpit-delivered English, spoken, sung.
Blame? Who's to blame? Or what's to blame? Language
Lives by its own slowly unfolding rules
And chance morphologies, its shapes, and age,
Its histories the same as the people's.
Cut out our tongues to save the national face?
Let language happen in its commonplace,
Its ordinary, extraordinary
Occasions of speaking, singing, and writing,
Whether by C. M. Grieve or J. M. Barrie,
Excoriating, plain, or else delighting.
What happens in languages happens – it's
Destructive to contest their inner wits
Propelled by how time dips phonology
In what gets left behind by big events
Or weather, or how people work and play,
Their pleasures, sorrows and their discontents.
Pictish, Gaelic, Norse, Scots rural sounds live
Even in altered voices, talkative
Survivals, fragments of noise, like place-names,
Those first poems in the crowded chronicle
Of the map of Scotland – a map proclaims
Languages' mix as ineradicable.
The onomastic mind looks into time,
Its one geography a named sublime.
    In our new Parliament, our accents mix
With confidence – get that into our lyrics!
No one's branded by a vocal stigma,
By mystical public schools or Oxbridge,
By England's creepy, sad, vocal enigma,

That patronising sound of patronage.
Now I hear children speak in a natural voice,
Accented zest and cadence. If it's choice
It's also nature. True to their time and place,
They show their mums and dads up, oldster frauds
Who buckled when their teachers set the pace
On how to speak (*'properly!'*), bawling the odds
Because we spoke the parish dialect,
Not junior BBC in our voice-wrecked
Pronunciation (so our teachers said).
Eagle, Hotspur, and *The Children's Newspaper,*
Wizard, Adventure, Daily Record, what I read
As a child made me no vocal leper nor
A local prig. I speak two ways, and write
In more than one, plural, and impolite.

    Live and let live. Promote the various.
Surrender to the spirit. Woodland. Moorland.
Put argument aside. Try to discuss.
Walk by the riverbank, and take your stand
By the midge-coloured water, the dark pools,
Rippling trout-rings. Watch the dozing owls.
That, too, is of our tongues, being our place,
Source of what strength we have, or character,
Wherever we came from or persisting trace
Of elsewhere lingering like a loyal spectre.

    Who legislates when Jock does something foul
To rolling consonantal R, or vowel,
Or lards his speech with epithets of F.
Well, we should. So, clean up your act. Turn down
The dreary, forthright volume, before we're deaf
From all that cursing from the angry town
And its intensifying Fs and Cs,
Indignant, crude monotonies!

What's the language of laughter? Or sorrow
When it's suffered in silence? Or a love-moan,
A sob and cry in the night? Such sounds borrow
Each other's commonplace from polyphone
Humanity. They do not need a word.
Who cares whose fingers run across the keyboard?
'A note don't care who plays it,' a wise man said.
And only an indifferent poem gets lost
In its translation. In my flowerbed
Most plants and shrubs aren't native but have crossed
Seas, seasons, different climates, to be here
Thriving in shaded Scottish horticulture.
One day I'll feel the confidence to grow
Orchids. But let my lilies flourish in
This land and tongue of rain and cloud-shadow.
Lilies and roses, too, are of this nation.

Ripe Bananas

After the dark morning, February blue
Shakes the dishevelled, lingering pods,
Resistant leaves, the mossed rose-tree.
Each day is longer now
By a few measurable minutes
Enough to contrive late afternoon
Or sun-over-the-yardarm.
Robins still roll through the cotoneasters
Or pose on the bird-feeder.
I notice how central heating protects
Surviving fruit flies. Ripe bananas
Show off their bruises. They'll last
Another day unless I eat them first
Or bake banana muffins.
A robin on a wheelbarrow puffs out its breast,
Show-off, and nasty with it.
As a member of the RSPB
I'm a bit disgusted by these bully robins.
A door shifts on a draught, a spider's lace
Moves on a puff that might just be my breath.
I can hear an oatcake crumble,
Tiny disturbances of dust and fluff,
Bubbles fizzing in
My Bombay-and-tonic,
This pencil on this paper.
Somehow, they're enough of noise
For a domestic symphony,
A solitude sufficiently robust
To encourage mumbles of wonder.